TIÁM
and songs of becoming

Kendra Marie
&
Steven James Schmidt

Copyright © 2018 by Steven Schmidt
All rights reserved. Thank you for buying an authorized edition of this book and for complying with copyright laws by not reproducing, scanning, or distributing any part of it in any form without permission.

ISBN: 978-1-7326533-0-6

Printed in the United States of America

Cover photo by David Cano

in all times and all places
in all seasons and feelings
You are
my forever love
my most cherished one

This is the authors' story of falling in love, a two-part collection documenting the private poems and letters exchanged during the course of their relationship and first year of marriage. It concludes with their wedding vows and two final poems.

CONTENTS

Tiám

awakening *3*

You held my hand *5*

You are everywhere *7*

i wait and i thirst *9*

a letter *11*

Beloved *13*

we can sleep when we're older *15*

spring *17*

You are the fire beneath *19*

name *21*

mystery *23*

pentecost *25*

rem|stage five *27*

calling *29*

songs *31*

stars *33*

everything is precious *35*

you are my night *37*

we will never stop being *39*

to love is to be taught *41*

follow me *43*

is Eternity really a matter of time? *45*

reunion *47*

my song of songs *49*

the way of a pilgrim *51*

candlelight *53*

after love *55*

seasons *57*

looking at you from across the room *59*

desire *61*

restore & redeem *63*

fire or ice *65*

You & God *69*

blueprints *71*

i think we'll be young forever *75*

odyssey *77*

don quixote *81*

unfolding *85*

covenant *87*

delight is a verb *89*

the exile *91*

time *93*

Becoming

Vows *97*

this morning *106*

tiám *107*

Tiám

awakening
—SJ

You woke me up
(You didn't know You did)
parched soul, thirsty for poetry
wretched soul, thirsty for grace.

You haven't left my side
(a clone is just as good)
tempted dreams, with keys and with doors
waking dreams, with conscience to mend.

why are You a song i can just comprehend?
why was i blind to the verses before?
the strangest and most beautiful blinders
are there for a time but removed at a cost.

surely i have paid the price
to feel such a tear, a divide:
You.

my grief reigns green instead of by grace
as the selfish and selfless intertwine,
becoming twins in the mirror of conscience.

the mirror is fogged
with the dew of this pretense,
yet there is somehow Beauty
in the verdict, fog, and obstruction:

the Selfless Divine intercedes on your behalf
to bring me back to sleep

again.

You held my hand
—SJ

we were boarding
a train for the future,
ticket in hand
and then
You handed me yours
and
held me:

not all of me, a part of me.
yet all of me.

and i am still here:
arm burning with
the unsaid, unknown, and petrifying mystery
of Why and If.

do i want the scourge to stop?
or do i want the scourge to seal?
i know i know i know
the Why and If and Answer
in my bones

but
will i ever christen the Mystery?

You are everywhere
—SJ

did You hear me today
as i whispered in the gentle breeze
with the words "i think of You"?

did You feel my touch
as i bartered with tense
of touch fulfilled?
were You aware of my fragrance,
the gentle spice caressing the words
of moments past?
were You aware of my ghost
lurking on the faces
of strangers and passersby?

i heard
i felt
i saw
and knew
You, even though i never
heard your whisper
felt your touch
or saw your ghost.

You were in nothing and
You were in everything:
the all inside the stillness.

i wait and i thirst
—SJ

i wait and i thirst

as i know and know not
the You in the depths and the shallows:
caresses and touches and currents
conspiring and knowing and drowning.

i would trade breath for the waters
that might pull me out into your wake:
pruning my skin and burning my eyes
with the salt of your sea and your essence.

oh that You would be the death
of me and my breath!

instead,
i cough You up
and gasp on rocks and faint,
falling upon the sand–tired and alone.

i thirst for You but You evaporate.
the last cells i can remember
return to their previous life,
leaving only the taste of tears behind.

maybe one day i will find the You i can breathe
and dive into the shallows, depths,
cracks, and nudges of earth and moon.

but for now i will subsist on
the beads trickling down my arms
and crashing into the corners of my body.

a letter
—SJ

My beloved,

I can barely sleep right now. You keep me awake even though you aren't with me.

I do not know what to do with this Torment. I ache and long for You. I am impatient and long for a time when I can give into these Passions and not keep myself from You. But the Ought takes precedence over Desire and Weakness, emotion and overwhelm. Circumstances hold me to a different a course and Loyalty holds me fast. I must wait even though I am tempted to rationalize myself away from the Ought and off of this course, this path, this code.

I long to blaze a different path, to rest in new pasture with You at my side. I long to imbibe in the Joy of Connection, Compassion, Loyalty, Growth, Faith, Humor and Wisdom of Us. These visions are the fruit of Temptation and I do not trust my own strength in their light.

The only path I can bear is admitting this weakness and naming my Passions for You. What else can I do when You, yourself, could name these Passions as easily as the stars?

You are not unaware, so I must honor your Knowledge. To withhold the Existence of these Passions for the sake of Friendship would be, for us, a Lie and the Death of Trust. I have no guilt in our Truth, but I lament my inability to Express this Truth in the ways I wish I could.

Our Expression is an issue of Time and Deed, so while I desire to share both, for the sake of Honor, I must limit that Time to specific contexts, and thereby chastise Us to specific Deeds. This Chastity is the source of my Torment.

But this Torment is not without its accompanying Joys. The more deeply I feel the sting, the more deeply I trust in the Depth. Whenever I choose Patience, I find more Strength.

If I must wait for You–and if the Waiting comes hand in hand with this Torment–then I welcome the Suffering as a Brother, with open arms and an open mind. Torment will be my Teacher and, perhaps, through this Education, I might one day become the Man worthy enough to call You his Companion and his Beloved.

Yours (all else is inexpressible)

Beloved
—KM

My beloved,

Passion, Wisdom, Chastity, Torment. These are Characters that drive an adventure worth taking.

You gave Passion a name, which seems only fitting because she is a quiet storm, a version of me that I now know only because you have led me to shake her hand. That touch has sent my entire being into her eye. A place of quiet, but an uneasy space filled with the tension of palpable stillness, as it pulls against my heart's inevitable motion. That one moment, that touch is a glimpse of the gorgeous rain that floods the world outside, though small in its components. A look here, a touch there, a moment spent fitting perfectly in Passion's arms letting her fingers traverse a desert of trust. I wait eagerly, impatiently even, to step across the threshold of passion's eye & be swept away & consumed by her wind. Breezes of her mighty hand tickle the outstretched branches of every thought I wake to. You are in the breeze, tempting me. I can hear you floating outside, touching the doors & windows, waiting to knock. It is here, in this moment that I will wait on you & wait on Him, because once I fall into Passion's embrace again, there will be no eye to run to. I will be blissfully & irrevocably consumed by the storm of you that has brewed.

You gave Wisdom a name, the respect it deserves. Wisdom is the man I want to meet over & over again. I wish to bow my head & submit every day as he gives me his name, even when I feel he's exhausted his breath. Let Wisdom then be the bridge from me to you. May Discernment stack Wisdom's bricks, with Patience as the mortar so that one day Wisdom might be the piece that defines Us as Us. Someday we will meet. We will cross from our beautiful islands & come together, standing on wisdom's sturdy arch having full trust in its construction & then, we will meet Wisdom together.

You gave Torment a name. You are right to welcome him. He is a worthy teacher, but his effect is intoxicating. He sits, twisting language together into lectures on longing & intimacy. He pokes & prods, setting himself in thoughts & dreams, moving from room to room as he has his effect on mouth & mind, body & emotion. It is equal parts addicting & freeing to sit with Torment. I wake at times heavy with the burden of wanting. It is Torment that sits with me in sleepless hours or lonely drives & he reminds me that right rarely means easy. He reminds me that sometimes it is more fulfilling to have to work for expression than it is to submit to whims of body, heart, & mind. Torment is my guide in these words. To somehow cage all of the things I am feeling, even into the constructs of language, is my dose today of Torment. He's met me here between these words & forced me into his embrace.

You are somehow managing to sweep me away, even at your distance. You're pulling me into a story full of Characters that I want to know & with visions of us that I want to experience. Let Passion, Wisdom, Chastity, & Torment all submit then, to Time. You do not walk a path of discernment alone. I pursue Faith, Love, Christ, & what is right alongside you, seeking to be a woman worth to be called Beloved.

we can sleep when we're older
—SJ

we can sleep when we're older:
when the darkness is no longer our communion
when the stars are no longer our brethren
when the moon is no longer our guide

when we are no longer babes
awake with the cries of new desire
when we are no longer children
awake with the signs of promise
when we are no longer youth
awake with the temptation of new worlds

when i am no longer a prisoner to your eyes
and set free by years of knowledge
when i am no longer bound to your hands
and set free by apollo's promise
when i am no longer chained to your chalice
and set free by the wine of the morn

when sleep is no longer my poison
when light is no longer our divorce
when communion is captive to eternity.

my muse and my love
my siren of old and new:
we can sleep when we're older.

spring
— KM

Come to me
my love and watch
as our winter wanes
combinations of light and seed
press against an icy horizon

Come to me
my love and watch
as our morning moans
the seal of night is broken
and prisms of you give way

Come to me
my love and watch
as the rain resuscitates
submit to its touch and blush
and heed the heightened color

Come to me
my love and watch
as our sleep surrenders
spring laughs for youth and wonder
and yawns to its prior

You are the fire beneath
—SJ

You were once the stillness of a moon-bathed lake.
You were once the stillness of winter,
life bottled up, preparing to spring.

then
the vibrations stirred us to the joys of love:
kisses, tender and serene
flickers and torrents of light
fingers gasping
lungs grasping for breath,
suffocating under the weight of the untold and unsaid
paralleled hearts in their relation and life
guiding us in rhythm and blood.

You were once the stillness my love
and someday You will return.

but for now
You are the fire beneath the cold, barren earth
and We are its keeper.

name
—SJ

words that once were weapons
are now maimed.
words that once held truth
are wrought with falsehood,
for no word can know
You.

what word can bear the responsibility?

mystery
—SJ

if a picture is worth a thousand words,
then surely you are the ocean.

pentecost
—SJ

our hearts ponder in two twilights,
theirs and ours
our brows furrow, tense and free
our mouths invite years of questions,
forged then fulfilled
our tongues speak wordlessly,
in breath and in fire
our eyelashes glance in the eyes of the storm
our feet share seconds and inches,
minutes and miles,
our legs snake through paradise, a verdant bed
our hands climb branches to the sky
then

our futures tease the kindling,
our pasts join in the embering,
and spirit stirs everything to
pentecost

our days to come calcify in the deep silence.
we caress the ashes away like children,
tossing them to the wind
where they will
forever be and
never be again.

rem | stage five
—KM

my dreams are jealous
of the reality of you
working overtime to create
moments of sweat and breath
that pale next to the sound of you
giggling between my sheets
body and soul tangled in love
my bed a battlefield of sleep and awake
a cemetery for dreams as they bow at your invasion
take them oh lord of mine as prisoner
they are subject to your touch
take them oh lord of mine as prize
the most worthy victor
accept the humble surrender
and take all of me, my dreams in tow
to wherever my heart will rest with yours

calling
—SJ

forget the fireside,
You will be my light.
forget its warmth,
i will be your comfort.
forget attire,
ours will be that of Eden.

let us forget the lists and their brethren.
You are the only responsibility i have today.

forget the world and its table,
i delight in *your* bounty.
forget words and sounds,
our purpose lies beyond them.
beyond the horizon,
beyond the firmament,
the skies beckon us to bed my love.
they invite us to communion–
do You not hear their groans?
even the rain has joined the plea
even Mother entreats us
even Father is begging.

my love;
we would be wise to listen.

songs
—SJ

the birds sing songs
inherent in identity
and bound to instinct.
no one taught them the notes
or showed them the rhythm–
they just knew.

i sing a song
inherently unknown
and bound to love.
i did not know the notes
or the rhythm before You
but now i do.

our melody has been written on my heart
and no Song is sweeter.

stars
—SJ

You were once a star in the void
until You were taken to the kiln
and fire wrapped You in love
and gave You a spirit

what mysteries rest in your bosom
what dust sleeps in your eyes
what galaxies trace through your blood
what light, what time is latched in your lungs

You are made from the sweetest of dust
the holy of ashes
and there is no other star
in the firmament shining purer

the veil has been torn
so i rest hand in hand
with the worlds, light, and mysteries
of past and future stars

everything is precious
—SJ

half-shadows, soft and delicate
kiss your moon-bathed skin.
You are asleep and the night is quiet,
interrupted only by crisp leaves and tender air.
the hum of the world is reduced to a whisper,
the earth turns gently, but like its core,
i am awake, stirred by the nudges of dreams.

the dreams call:
be quick and be silent
wake and see
a jewel is slipping out of your grasp
so i awake

to an angel
outside of Time and Age.

You are youth and merit
humming along with the night.
your hair does not know my breath
your shoulders are numb in stillness
and your lips only know the taste of dreams.

i wish i were the shadows
flying and skimming the breadth of your skin:
surveying the curve of your breasts
the contours of your legs
the bends and breaks of your arms

the wells of your neck
and the fountain of your youth
but,

your slumber is holy
and deed becomes bound to rest.
i do not lament being turned to stone,
for whilst fire is brewing in my bones
i know it can wait.

dreams did not wake me for deed,
they woke me to know:
to heal my ignorant eyes of a blindness,
to understand
that each hum of your breath
and beat of your heart
is lost in the cavern of night and Time
and the losing is precious and vast.

our bodies will fade
and my countenance may fail in its brevity,
but the image of you in this night will endure.
my waking touched memory and turned it into gold:
a totem i will never lose and forever redeem.

you are my night
—KM

you are my night

memories bead and melt under the heat of my heart's
work and the body's immediate response

my nerves echo this and twitch
in quiet torment
waiting to touch and be touched

my addiction never wanes
in constant withdrawal
my body arrests your lips in hunger
their touch quenches
as they follow paths of passion
from head to heart to body
they leave rivers of satisfaction in their wake
to direct our adventure

you & I

we traverse the mountains of us
we carve mazes together
carefully mapping out constellations
telling stories the worlds pass as myth

I am the princess
fought and won by you
waiting faithfully for your return

delicately being prepared for the night
I might become your queen

my own body lies in wait
while your name sweetly ferments on my tongue
that one day the wait will end and I might drink you in
allowing all that you are to intoxicate my being

for now
you are my night
my slumber and my rest

but wait until I am awake...

we will never stop being
—SJ

today i feel a peace
unlike any i've ever known.

for months and moons
i waited with baited breath:
i knew a truth in my heart
and craved for it to be made word.

it was truth before and it is truth now
but it has changed form:
from vapor to water.
it has been filtered by tongue
and emerged holy and pure.

at long last i can see the clearing
and i fall to my knees,
worshiping the sight.
i would live here for millennia
were it not for the mountains begging to be crossed
and the oceans begging to be charted.

let us travel slowly towards that horizon.
let us bide our time in the water and woods.
let us stop for whispers a million times more.
let us take heart,
knowing the future is a
a fate named Us.

to love is to be taught
—SJ

we will make a house on the beach
and there we will purge by sand.
the currents will wash our nature away
until all that is left is spirit.
the weeds will tangle and join us in the dance.
new life will burrow our land
and come alongside us.
the rocks will cry out with us
to a maker
and salt will settle on the coast
of our wine.

they will all be our guests at the banquet
and there will be no more secrets.

let us sing join creation
in the language of the earth
and partake in the bounty of
limbs and chills,
turns and tides,
potions and praise.

we are loyal hosts, mother,
and we invite you in:

come, teach us lessons and myths!
we are your vessel to fill to the brim.
bring the means and we are the altar!

bring the moans and we will tear!
bring the mistakes and we will heal!

let us share and trade what we have
in our home by the sea.

follow me
—KM

follow me to nowhere
lie with me to watch the world spin
find a path to nothing
with everything at its end

on our backs we wait
pointing at vapor, stealing rays from the sun
daring the rain to wash us away
seeking the lives we've won
a pillow as our prize
your voice a final call
to dreams where blushes gather
and wait for wishes to fall

no cage to bind our breath
no where for hopes to hide
all stripped naked at your feet
bowing humbly to their pride
the wind we make is mighty
to send the past away
the breeze that is left is quiet
kissing laughter on its prey

the stars we have lit are angry
for what they cannot capture
Time holds Promise in its shadows
with Patience wrapping tighter

follow me to everywhere
dance with me to help the world stop
let us lose ourselves to everything
and let Forever eavesdrop

is Eternity really a matter of time?
—SJ

she tempts him with Forever whilst the
vapors shade the sun. he says
"fall is not yet here, my love, and
spring has just begun."

Patience binds the Promise and the
Harvest to a Time, much like
all of his attempts to find the
truth within a rhyme.

the trying might be foolish when held
captive to a word, but
the Novice rests assured for it is
Word he's never learned.

Word and Time were finite till he
joined her on the path we call
Eternity (unknown amidst the
western way of wrath).

Now they hold a Future—
fingers meet, they understand:
Eternity is shared within the
palm of their one hand.

reunion
—SJ

i can see your visage
glistening like a golden jewel
steadfast in loyal beauty.

i can see your mirror in the firmament
a mirage in what was once barren.
then

> the trees clap their hands
> the birds' song is sweeter
> the earth joins the singing
> the grass chatters
> the sky cries in joy

everything knows

> my roots know – the spring is full to the brim
> my heart knows – it pounds in the silence
> my cheeks know – they blush at the thoughts
> my body knows – it aches and groans
> my mind knows – sleep held no respite

> > the dust is shaken off
> > the weeds are pulled out
> > the mountains move
> > the fire is kindled
> > the table is set.

everything knows
and all is prepared
for the reunion
of me and my love.

my song of songs
—SJ

      your hair is a crown—feathers of gold
      (refined by the sun and the wind)
      brushing

      your eyes—doves
      (of ocean, current, change, storms, and foam)
      flying above

      your cheeks—jewels
      (blushed red in the light of the morning sun)
      bordering

      your mouth—a gate of Eden
      (home to the sweetest of fruits)
      framed by

      your lips—honey
      (soluble in essence, sprouting buds and butterflies)
      dripping down

      your neck—a plain
      (of wheat and maize)
      dancing on

      your shoulders—havens and hills
      (thrones and fields of grace)
      framing
      your breasts—mountains

(guides on an eager horizon)
giving birth to

your navel—a pool of vapor
(glistening as glass and cool to the touch)
sustaining

your hips—wild mares
(waking by the waterside)
galloping down

your legs—trails of amber
(and pillars of marble)
ending at

your feet—precious wings
(five-feathered and strong)
waking our wind

the way of a pilgrim
—SJ

i am a pilgrim,
new to these lands,
yet sovereign

over the mountains and trails,
the pools and the plains,
the havens and hills.

i am both
benevolent ruler and humble traveler
making my way back to the start.

the journey is patient:
in the motion of the reigning,
in the chills of fire,

until patience dies
and the victor is passion–
the siege has begun.

caverns and castles convene,
turrets pine for the sky,
and we become sinews and strength.

vapors invade the plains,
honey floods the land,
and the current creates a blur of bliss.
the pools and plains,

the havens and hills
shake and tremble.

the earth quakes in knowledge
and
at last
we are undone...

we drift.

serene ships
in a sea of soul.

candlelight
—SJ

the candles dance on your skin
caressing your glow with theirs
so that You become a goddess

You burn with fire
You crackle
You twist and turn
a phoenix of passion
an ember or earnestness

this light will never fade
and You will never die

after love
—SJ

subtle sighs and eyes closed.
seconds rhyming with the silence.
the earth reversing.
eden restoring.
no weight in time.
the stillness sustaining.
eternity

seasons
—SJ

i had only known winter
in the guise of
spring, summer, and fall.
it was a hidden death,
an impostor, a judas, a vulture
tongued in silver and beaked in bribe.
though this betrayal has a welcome identity
it has been marked as Trojan times
and prior seed.

but You

You opened my eyes to other seasons:
new life, heat, flowers, harvest.

now i
now We
live in this new entity:

a season of blue eternity with
life, heat, flowers, and harvest all together,
spinning in touches and tongue and tangles
and rumors and rapture and ransoms
and crosses and keeping and crowds.

all my mistakes melt together into miracle
and the shadow of death melts away to mirage.

i had only known winter,
but now We follow in the wake of them all.

looking at you from across the room
—SJ

You don't feel my eyes glancing the back of You as You read. You have entered your book and You are in your mind, discovering new worlds, precepts, and questions and it is quiet. your head is bowed down and your legs are crossed, set across the high table in front of You.

one day there will be miles and memory between us
instead of mere minutes and margins.
there will be years in your hands
and stories on your tongue,
youth in your soul and sage in your temple,
cracks in your skin and wounds near your heart.

who knows
the bounties and the scarcities we will have shared,
the sacrifice and relent we will have endured,
the covenant and the cords,
the word and the vows,
service and searches,
latches and locks,
markets and matches,
keys, boxes,
kisses, battles,
houses, homes,
loves, languages,
and lives we will have lived?

i do know one thing:
even after all of it,
your legs will still be crossed
and your head will still be bowed,
taking in the sentences and sentiments of the world.

and i will still be glancing You.

desire
—SJ

i want to be the footsteps
in your wake.

i want to be the seed
you spread.

i want to be the breath
in your sighs.

i wish i was everything
closest to You.

restore & redeem
—SJ

i am a prisoner
with no need for parole.
i chose this sentence
in a thousand dreams before and
will in a thousand dreams hence.

color me a culprit of love tomorrow
that i might live my life out
chained to your chalice
and bound to your bosom
as i did in this day.
frame me a burglar of beauty
and bring the gavel down again—
i find welcome within your walls
and grace within your gates.

O my love, imprison me:
your life be my sentence!
You are the court
and justice is due.

fire or ice
—KM

on your lips
where my breath
my word
and my heart reside
a question dances:
fire or ice?
somewhere between those perilous pillows
lies my sanity
resting in its naivety

just when I have concluded that they are fire
when their touch has scorched every inch of my body
engulfed in white hot flicks
the breath they took from me
dancing between us like licks of light
representations of a soul consumed
wildly
furiously
with no hope for containment
just when I have concluded that they have stolen
all of the air my lungs could ever hope to create
when I think they've left me to return to the earth
as I came
a dazzling carbon
happily conceding to be dust
you touch them to mine again and I
freeze.
the coolness of you causes hair to rise

and mountains of lust to rise upon my skin
flags
waving their surrender
to your word
to your deed
to your whim

your kisses
flakes upon my ground
falling softly
tantalizingly slow
no one like its prior
each one more intricate and delicate than the last

leaving a sheer blanket of you on all that I am
your dusting leaves the world quiet

a deafening silence filled with the mysterious laughter
a half smile
an unfinished sentence from the fire before

your elements continue to shape and move my body
the disaster of you begins to feel the most natural
you've brought beauty from ash
the most subtle form of alchemy
transforming all that's been created with your magic
I do not care
lips be fire or ice, rain or sun,

wind or eye, rock or water
only let them touch me again that I might reside
in whatever force you are
that I might find my sanity.

You & God
—SJ

it is in the space–
the lack–
i become aware of all that is.

every step between us,
every mile of earth and sky,
every wall, mountain,
ocean and valley

is Us:
an emptiness
fully in bloom.

blueprints
— KM

i've built you a house
carefully designed
penned by a artist
that i long to control
she is me
but i know her not
she was birthed
conceived outside of my own
but i submit to her design
in love
a foundation of patience
rushed into being
drawn by unknown Hands
meeting walls of trust
constructed overnight
while sleep stole me away
windows with curtains of emotion drawn
letting in gradual light
as my horizon breaks
and sun awakes
a roof of faith
gathering shingles
holding rains of fear

inside i placed my soul
the deep of me living
in the shallow of us
a maze of me for you to solve

each room stacked with clues
riddles of past present future
with no destination in mind
except our new additions
hidden in prose
colored by language
forged by story

you stalk from room to room
tiptoeing around corners
that are yours to barrel through
knocking on doors
that are yours to enter into

but you
glorious you
instead you delicately dance
through blueprints utterly affected by you
asking before you enter
giving each room the respect and silence it deserves

you sit and meditate with me all around you
not realizing that this room
each room
was built for you to sit in
crafted with you in mind
this is why
your feet send the room into its fullness

the whole house groans for your breath
longs for your feet
as the final piece in its design
the element we didn't know we needed

stay your course
o wanderer
traipse through your mystery
touching walls and opening doors
continuing down halls
and turning on lights

for this house
this maze
is yours as much as mine

i think we'll be young forever
—SJ

we are young in what we know.
the tastes of spring are fresh on our lips,
the colors new.
the breeze carries seeds—gentle kisses
bearing and flying the flags of futures.
our youth tempts in a neverland guise,
but youth is merely the sowing of wonders,
not the reaping.

the harvest is in the transformation:
when the blues and greens mix
in the middle ground of red and gold,
when the ice marries the wind,
when fires blaze in the heart,
when the steady stream of winter's end
courses down the drive,
and when the sweet caress has no rise or fall–
simply the prestige of a promise.

Spring is now
and we are forever.
Change is our champion,
transformation our trade,
and my joy rests in the in-between.

odyssey
—SJ

>we speak in the smallest of seeds,
>in the tiniest of whispers,
>in the slightest touch,
>like the summer night air.

>You are a flower in my hand,
>tender and delicate,
>dancing upon holy water,
>gliding, caressing the surface of the deep.

>You are precious and small,
>a perfect diamond,
>carbon concentrated by time and age,
>pure in the light, both fire and brimstone.

>we are nucleus, centered and whole.
>then the night beckons us.
>the nucleus of silence is shattered
>and we react:

>a friction charged by the lightning of space,
>we tease the earth with fire and charge the sky.
>clouds form and holy water pours down

>and You cradle the storm:
>your flowers dance in the rain,
>your diamond is set alight.
>i am hephaestus, and You, aphrodite:

playing with fire like a toy,
forging the weapons of love
in the blind euphoria of creation.

we morph into ares, riding into battle:
drums pounding in the deep,
athena as a witness, weeping
for how cleverly we wield wisdom.

surely, other mortals could not
withstand the gravity of *this*.
so the question is worth asking:
have we become immortal?

You invincibly endure the refining
as i steal You again and again:
purging impurities, washing in water,
locking in lightning, and forging in fire.

the storm rages and the earth joins the dance,
torrents fall and ocean flood,
waves break, the earth quakes
and *at last* we bear the burden of the end.

we return to mortality
with our shard of eternity,
but this is only the eye of our storm
the calm is false, the abating a lie.

we will return
to the earth and the sky
for this is but the eye,
my love,

and we will storm again
when it passes us by.

don quixote
—KM

knowing eyes making mazes
from feet
to hands
to lips
to collar
scared to meet
the table a race
the space between as wide as a
few words
rooted in the mind but tapping on
the tongue

we took our communion
gave ourselves to body & blood
a promise of tonight
but a taste
a question of forever

and our dance began
as he fell into his dream
where everything he read
the stories of princes & choices
of kisses
of romance
of courtly promises
the deluge of love at first touch
all that he lost his sanity to

he wished into reality
it became the mission in his trance

we joined in his fall from the
sensible
tension twirling & leaping between
hands
hearts

our thoughts spinning & meeting
palm to palm before being
whisked away

as we fell into his story
we lost our minds to ours as well

the idea that all we've dreamt
might be found while awake
that all the tales from pages &
knees
could be choreographed into
one heart
one look
one word
one man

you are the man
the prince of my personal mania

& I have been lost
enchanted by our reality
hypnotized in the gentleness
of trust
mesmerized by our sweet
confessions
beguiled by your word
penned in the language of me
living
captivated by your love
given so freely
without the heels of expectation
to punch holes in the foundation
that we glide across

your strength & your wisdom
a firm support
you've taught me the trust
i require to fly

send me soaring
out of that dream
into now
and let us bend low to the
applause of fate
in humility for its compulsion
in pride for our production
send me back to that table

where i might drink you in
& our dream may begin again.

unfolding
—SJ

the wake of our life enfolds entire worlds.

silent, secret streams
only *our* bodies have danced in
vast, breathing fields
only *our* fingers have laughed across
old, wise hills
only *our* spines have whispered to

great stone mountains erupt from our solitude
into the canyons of memory,
weaving in and out of heaven
until all we have lived is dreaming.

covenant
—SJ

we are adam and eve
with no serpents in sight

only the trees will watch the rings of our years
and only the bees will taste
the sweet perfumes of our nectar,
the precious honey from our lips

O earth, we will mend your broken parts,
strewn among thorns and threshing floors!
come, every bud to be christened,
we will give you a name!

we are family,
formed long ago
in the mind of God,
and we will leave you
dancing within the wind

delight is a verb
— SJ

look at You:
the pearls dangling down,
a crown of gold
i can brush and hold and forge.

your crown is your mind:
beautiful, precious,
an emblem of your dignity,
an altar i can worship.

your eyes are your soul:
transforming in the frame,
crystal and ocean dancing
in the light of an intrinsic sun.

your word is your heart:
thoughtful, patient,
and savored by those wise enough
to know the taste of such sweetness.

your flowers are heaven:
a gate, an opening to eternity
and all that might ever be.

You are more than lightning:
trapped in tiny bursts and seconds.
You are more than particles:
bound in a mystical magnetism.

You are a tapestry,
a womb of spirit.

You are a truth:
whispering in the quiet,
gentle pulsing of stillness.

let us delight in your truth:
wrapping vines around our waists,
luring ourselves in, and
fulfilling the promises we made to each other.

my love, my love, my love
let us delight
in Love.

the exile
—KM

o Heart

punish me if you must.
my soul sends treasonous beams
raging for his beat above yours

o Breath

punish me if you must.
hold yourself captive
your caverns rise and fall with his inhale

i am guilty
mad with love
resigned to pay

send me to service
lay me at his feet
indentured

no

shackle me to his words
binding me as his muse
enraptured

no
beat me with his smiles

reaching his eyes as the final blow
unconscious

no
scourge me with his lips
leaving trails of heat
body weak

no
torture me with whispers
trembling at their touch
unhinged

and if this is not sufficient
exile me
banish me away to blissful life
his soul with mine
the sentence
i leave my heart and my breath on the shore
to be washed away on the island of Us.

time
—SJ

you are a feeling,
like a watch I used to wear.

you are still here
> *keeping time*
> *staining my skin*
> *a warm, feathered breeze*
> *an absinthe kiss*
> *an absence*
> *gilding the smallest pores and*
> *chased in what were and would*
> *(and will) be.*

you dissolve
> *into my blood*
> *carving initials on the walls of my veins*
> *parading about to an unwitting crowd*
> *singing back*
> *swimming back*
> *to the source*
> *of it all.*

you are the only time I know.

Becoming

Vows
- SJ -

My beloved,

When I think about the larger, mystical forces at work here—God, Love, Family, Friendship—words hardly seem capable of true and honest expression. When I contemplate our Love, this Commitment, and everything this day signifies, again words fail me.

While falling in love with You, there were times I felt a similar sense of awe, a similar sense of bearing witness to something sacred and precious. Mostly, they occurred in quiet moments when I would look into your eyes and it was as if I could see a universe of love expand within them. It was a like a world of You torn from a veil: hidden, yet seen, intimate and infinite in its proportions.

Humanity has spent countless time philosophizing, contemplating, and creating this thing we call Love. And yet, we are nowhere closer to knowing its depths or understanding its currents. We have not fully grasped its strength, nor witnessed the extent of its world-bending power. It is a strange, profound, and endless Mystery.

Even though my expression of Love is metaphorical at best, the power of this day is found in the awareness that Love is not actually a Mystery to any of us. When I look at You, Kendra, it is not a metaphor or turn of phrase, it not an intellectual idea or some ethereal thing. When I look out at all of you, our dear friends and family, I am reminded of the millions of moments you each embodied this Mystery, and taught me that Love is grounded and steadfast instead of a feeling or passing state of being. I was taught love through the presence of my friends, the support of my family, the companionship or unexpected kindness of a stranger. I was taught by all of you that Love can be experienced in a beautiful sky, a warm home, or a crashing wave.

And this is the Love I have for You, Kendra Marie–a Love more than any words, even the vows I am about to take. It is a Love I learned *from* You, a Love I witness every time I look into your eyes and somehow know that You love me like no one else ever has. I look into your eyes and am humbled because You see me, You know me, and miraculously still want to hang out with me forever.

However, I am most thankful that our Love is not naive. It is not young, ethereal, or at the mercy of the Tides of Life. Though we do not know much, we realize that Life is a strange, beautiful series of dichotomies and unexpected turns, and no matter our intentions for this day or the vows we take, that neither will result in a perfect life or a perfect marriage. We both know that the strength of these vows lie in the Truth that Love is inexplicably intertwined with the frustrations, drudgeries, successes, heartbreaks, joys, and sufferings of Life.

And I want *all* of these with You.

I want a lifetime of coffee cups, stupid faces, broken plates, tears, knowing smiles, take-out Thai food, angry tirades, ambitions realized, failures endured, long flights, cups of ramen, crying babies, blonde hairs in the drain, too many books, and RuPaul reruns. I want inside jokes and empty bottles of wine, friends laughing too loud, and awkward, peaceful stillness.

Kendra Marie, as we embark on this journey, these are the vows I pledge to You.

I vow:

> To never let someone else physically or emotionally invade or violate the space between us.
>
> To always say cute things that make You want to make out with me.
>
> To be honest and work through conflict, no matter, how much I want to be passive aggressive, sarcastic, or generally avoid it like the plague.
>
> To ask questions and be endlessly curious with You about Everything.
>
> To pursue God to the ends of the Universe with You.
>
> To contemplate the life of Jesus and seek to live and love You as He lived and loved on this Earth.
>
> To do everything in my power to make You feel seen, heard, respected, honored, and cherished.
>
> To forgive and forget what we must let go.

To forgive and remember when it helps us grow.

To ask for forgiveness.

To forgive myself when I make mistakes.

To be humble and never lose sight that neither of us is perfect.

To love You through sacrifice, servant-hood, and selflessness.

Lastly, I vow to never take You or any of this for granted, and to approach every moment we share with eternal thanks and gratitude simply because You are there.

Kendra, You have changed everything for me: the way I see, the way I hear, the way I speak, the way I think, the way I feel. Here is a to a lifetime of continuous change. Here is to whatever Life will bring.

Vows
- KM -

My beloved,

April 18, 2016.

I decided to start writing this now. To begin slowly filing away careful and deliberate words so that this chaos of sounds bursting from the corners of my brain find their way to a page. I desperately need my vows to be active, moving, breathing, past, present, and future, so that they will always be more than idyllic memories. I started this now so that our love would be more than just a destination and that this day would not be inviting others to see a peak devotion, but instead, welcoming others in to an ever changing redemption story woven together by hands bigger than ours. I know I love you now, but I hope that this love, today, will seem small tomorrow, that our love would blossom, our capacity to love with it, in tandem. I started this now so that I can have a record of every time you absolutely failed to meet my expectations.

Where I expected confusion and chaos you brought clarity and discernment. Where I expected time and healing to sludge by you came rushing in destroying the sandcastles of cynicism and pain I had carefully crafted. Where I expected you to see a lack, instead you found abundance. Where I expected walls to go up, you found a way to not smash them down, but to delicately craft a window perfectly shaped to the eyes of your soul where we could meet day in and day out spending hours looking inside trusting that patience would one day open the door. I started it now just in case we have forgotten how it feels to have a friend willing to fall, jump even, into gray areas of "I don't know", whether we find the answer or end up with more questions than we started with.

April 29, 2016.

The first time you told me you loved me, I thought I heard wrong. You opened your mouth and the trio of words flew out in chaotic counterpoint weaving around my brain trying to find a place to root themselves. In that moment, I had a better understanding of the power of these three words. I've learned the selfishness in the "I" is the ability to say confidently with the humility that comes with being broken, that in divine image, I stand complete. I am a strong, capable woman who holds creativity, intelligence, spirituality, and a unique voice. Second, the understanding that "love" means saying yes to what is and that loyalty, honesty, and fight, but surrender when the time comes are all a part of accepting that "what is" is enough.

But now I've come to "you." Since that moment I have spent countless hours pondering the mystery of you, in awe of everything you are. In awe of everything that I am and become because I know you. You have taken over. Every thought I have about my future is seen through glasses tinted by the colors of us, of you and me, Steven James.

This day cannot come soon enough.

May 18, 2016.

Three years ago I wrote about love, but in a much different way. It was the first piece of my heart that I let you read. Right now I hope to amend it. I hope that I can, with the same eloquence, ruin my own plea. You are new evidence pointing to the fact that love is not guilty of the destruction that I once wrote of. That love is worth these vows. I have put you on the stand to testify and you have won love's case. I spoke of love first as paralyzing the will by limiting dreams. Steven James since the day you spoke a "yes" into our love story, dreams have taken form and come to fruition at such a rate that I can barely touch them as they whisk by. I sit, surrounded by the wind of possibilities for life that is swirling around us and I vow now to let our dreams continue to embrace us and push us together.

I spoke second of love soiling the Spirit and hindering faith. Love, the siren tempting me, the Odysseus, with beauty, but only masking a hideous face. You are my Penelope, waiting faithfully for my return from skepticism and doubt. I come home to your arms now knowing that our spirits combined are dynamite. That together, we have a hue of light that is unique. To separate you from me would be to dim and mute the light we have been given. It is for this reason I vow to give myself, not only to you as my husband, but also to the power of God in us. My light alone is no longer sufficient for I can love and serve better and more fully just by being with you.

I claimed emotions as love's next victim. It is here that we find our glorious paradox. I think being with you will always be equal parts terrifying and elating. Somehow we live between being absolutely overtaken by each other and the simplicity of being "right." Between glorying in our independence and still finding ourselves at the end of the day desiring to lay it down for the sake of being with the other. We live in the glorious space between young love and great love. We are new, but the love we've found is a buried treasure that I firmly believe only a handful of people will get in their lives, only because they'll never know to look for it. I vow to glory in our paradox, resting in our "rightness", yet continuing to search for ways to love you.

I've never wanted a person to complete me. I believe the lack that I have is holy. To complete me would fill in my cracks of light and I would become stone. I realize now that I've only ever wanted to find a soul to touch mine. Minds and bodies change and I might be saying, "I will" to someone who looks and thinks very differently in 10 years or 50 years, or tomorrow. In fact, I hope I do. I hope I wake up in days to come to a completely different person, not because you are lacking now, but because I have such hope in what you are becoming. The soul, though, is the core of a person, the unchanging. And oh have I fallen for yours. I have fallen not because I know the full extent of your soul. Rather, I have fallen *because* I know I will never reach the end. You have become infinitely knowable. Your soul the subject of my curiosity, the thing I want to spend my entire life learning and experiencing. My vows to you today are not to your body, not to your mind, not even to your spirit, although I offer all of these things to you freely and completely, but to your soul.

It is for this reason that I ask you now to bend your breath around your name and mine, around our names as one. You have moved beyond a scribbled note in the margin, beyond a page, and beyond a chapter in my story. You are such a fundamental part of my ever-working narrative that I want to put your name in my title. I beg you to weave your legacy with mine that we might follow each other through it leaving hope and love and the Spirit in our wake. I will fold my mind into an envelope of us. Tucking in pieces only meant for you and sealing it with a kiss. I promise to mold my body to yours only as we leave this sacrament in oneness and continue the divine dance, in marriage, and in each other that we've sought together.

But above all, I vow to turn and shape my soul toward yours reaching past my eyes as they stare into yours, past words that I say now that declare you my husband, past hands that I will hold in tragedy or triumph, past the breaths that we are given, few or many. Near or far, arguing or laughing, our souls are holding hands. I vow to balance on this covenant. It is to these tethers that I will cling to. These tethers are what I weld into place now: the tethers of my soul to yours.

I love you forever.

this morning
—SJ

this morning,
we barely opened our eyes before
sleepily finding each others' lips like a first drink of water,
our fingers tracing the bed like there are no boundaries–
> *which there aren't.*

this morning,
we said hi to the grey morning sky,
and hurriedly found a kiss like an unexpected pearl,
still laced on our mouths like word–
> *which You are.*

this morning,
we ushered each other close to speak of love
before speech ever entered the fray.

this morning,
we were beckoned to sing a song
before notes ever entered the day.

this morning,
years were there and gone
in the skies and morns and words and songs of infinity.

> *my forever love,*
> *my most cherished one:*
> *two years*
> *and years of forever*

tiám

or the twinkle in your eye when first meet someone

—KM

let there be light.
    fluttered lids
    sleepy windows
and there was light.
    a subtle turn of lips
    closing the space of shadows
and it saw that it was good.
    awake and
    human and
    ours
it called the light day
    a cosmic event given in ecstasy
    embodied stars.
it called the absence night
    companion of wholeness
    beautiful and
    necessary.
there was evening and morning
    showing up as a twinkle
as I meet love in person
    day one.

ABOUT THE AUTHORS

Steven James Schmidt is an award-winning writer, musician, and educator. He is currently developing two musicals, a play, and teaches at Balboa Magnate Elementary School and the Los Angeles Children's Chorus.

Kendra Marie Schmidt is an avid reader, thinker, and photographer interested in psychology, theology, and women's studies. She holds a BM in Music Business from Azusa Pacific University and plans on pursing a doctorate in clinical psychology.

They live in Pasadena, CA.

You can follow Kendra on
Facebook | We Are Embodied.
Instragram | @kendyschmidt

You can follow Steven on
StevenJamesSchmidt.com
Facebook | sjschmidtmusic
Instagram | @sjschmidtmusic

www.ingramcontent.com/pod-product-compliance
Lightning Source LLC
Chambersburg PA
CBHW060459080526
44584CB00015B/1477